Unlock the ⟨
of
Manifesting
28 Day Journal

Unlock the Magic
of
Manifesting

28 Day Journal

Emma Kate Dawson

Published by Fuzzy Flamingo 2020
© 2020 Emma Kate Dawson

ISBN: 978-1-9161147-8-4

A CIP catalogue record for this book is available from the British Library

Cover design, typesetting and editing: Fuzzy Flamingo
www.fuzzyflamingo.co.uk

For Dad, thank you for introducing me to the Law of Attraction
For Mum, thank you for helping me to learn the darkest hour is the one before dawn, to get dressed and show up on the tough days, that I'm stronger than I realised and for the endless cups of tea, they mean more than I could ever say

Welcome to your
Unlock the Magic of Manifesting
28 Day Journal

I am so excited that you have decided to spend the next 28 days learning more about how you can co-create the life of your dreams and manifest with ease. Whatever has drawn you to buy this journal, trust that it is part of the divine plan; now is your time to explore the beautiful process of co-creation with the universe and *Unlock the Magic*.

A Quick Hello

Before you dive in, I want to take a quick moment to introduce myself. I'm Emma, Life & Mindset Coach for women who are ready to claim their Manifesting Queen crown to create the life of their dreams with less hustle and more flow. I'm here to help you reconnect with your authentic self, clear resistance, nurture a positive mindset, and manifest with ease and grace.

Wherever you are in life right now and whatever it is that you want to manifest into your reality, I know that it is entirely possible for you, because I have used the Law of Attraction to completely transform my life. Please don't for one minute think I'm perfect at this, or that I have a special given gift – I'm not and I don't! I'm just someone who saw another way of living life and decided to give it all I've got.

It wasn't so long ago that I was a single mum living on benefits, wondering how my life had fallen apart so rapidly. It was February 2013 when I received two things that would change my life forever: Confirmation that my divorce to husband 1.0 was finalised, and a copy of Rhonda Byrne's *The Secret*. I had very mixed feelings about the first thing and was seriously sceptical about the second! I'd always tried to be positive but a serious lack of self-confidence had kept my life pretty uninspiring.

Could I really change my life just with my thoughts? To be honest it all sounded a bit far-fetched.

But, I was sad, depressed, lonely, and looking for a way to build a new life alone, so I gave it a go.

Tentatively I started my first ever gratitude journal, and it changed my whole world.

To start with, the words I wrote felt begrudging; was I really grateful for my small and damp house after having to leave my beautiful home? Did I really feel thankful for the endless hours I spent looking after two very young children alone? But I wrote it all anyway and tried my best to feel it. Then things started to shift, small changes at first. I felt happier and lighter than I had for years – maybe forever – even though nothing in my external world was different. My bond began to deepen with my girls, my relationship with my ex-husband and his new girlfriend improved, I found the perfect part-time job, new friends, and a lovely little home for me and my daughters.

And that was just the start.

Since that day in February 2013 when I picked up my pen to start my first gratitude journal, I've manifested husband 2.0 (a BIG improvement on the first version!), our dream home, the perfect car, a new sofa, the most gorgeous dog, clients, money... So many amazing things.

I use the Law of Attraction for everything, from helping my day go smoothly to solving problems, finding perfect car parking spaces to reaching my soulmate clients.

It's not always been an easy ride and learning to master my mindset has been VERY challenging. There have been many times when I have been on the struggle bus facing frustration, blocks, and resistance, and that has led to some very deep personal development work. I've healed, released, forgiven, and changed more mindset BS than I would have believed it possible for one person to do.

Now, though, I'm so grateful that I did. Not only has this journey greatly improved mine and my family's lives, it's also led me to become the Life and Mindset Coach I am today with a dream business where I get to work with beautiful heart-centred women to help them transform their lives too.

If you'd like to learn more about the work I do, please visit:
www.emmakatedawson.com

I am so excited for you to have chosen this journal and to immerse yourself in learning all about how you can use the Law of Attraction to create the authentic and abundant life you're dreaming of.

Let's dive in.

What is Manifesting?

Simply put, manifesting is using the Law of Attraction to consciously bring what you want into your physical reality.

There are lots of myths that surround manifestation. It isn't simply visualising what you want and then waiting for it to drop out of the sky, nor is it lots of 'woo woo' rituals, or even hustling and controlling all the time to force what you want into your life.

Manifesting is actually a very simple process of asking for what you desire, getting into alignment with that desire, taking inspired action, and being open to receive.

It's all too easy to block what you want when you try to control, force, and hustle it into existence. Learning how to consistently manifest anything is learning to let go of *everything* that causes resistance, fear, doubt, and worry so that you can get into alignment with your authentic, higher self.

It is learning to trust in a power far greater than yourself, a power that you might intuitively feel, but don't fully understand or even believe in right now. It is building your faith in that power so you have certainty that you will be guided to the opportunities, people, and inspired actions that will bring your dreams to reality.

Manifesting is not so much something that you do, as who you become

This 28 day journal will guide you step-by-step through simple daily tasks to connect with authentic desires and get into energetic alignment. It will help to clear any resistance or doubt so that you can allow the Universe to work her magic and you too can manifest with ease.

Here are few things that will help you throughout the next 28 days...

Each task will fall into one of three main types: Affirmations, Action Prompts, and Journaling Prompts. Some of these I suggest that you repeat as Daily Mindset Rituals.

Commit to a time each day when you'll tackle the day's task. If morning doesn't work for you then find a time that does. Most of the tasks will take between 5 and 15 minutes and there are some that you will repeat each day, so I suggest setting aside 30 minutes per day. If that feels a lot, remind yourself *why* you want to learn how to Manifest with ease and that your dreams and goals matter.

Relax and have fun! Manifesting is a beautiful and amazing process that works so magically when you lean into joy. So above all, enjoy the next 28 days.

Let's Unlock The Magic of Manifesting.

DAY 1

Appreciation Rampage

Gratitude is a powerhouse when it comes to unlocking the magic of manifesting, in fact it is the corner stone, so we're starting here.

The more you appreciate the things you have in your life, the more good things you'll attract into your life.

Think of yourself baking a batch of cupcakes and giving them to young children. If they snatch, whinge about not having enough, and moan about how they could have been better, you don't feel inclined to give them any more.

But for the child who thanks you and tells you how yummy they were and how much they loved them, well that child you're happy to offer the whole plate to!

The Universe works in exactly the same way, so it's time to lean into gratitude in a BIG way.

Free write about everything – big and small – that you have to be thankful for. Here are some prompts to get what Abraham Hicks calls your 'Appreciation Rampage' started:
- Everyday things
- Special things
- People in your life
- People you don't know but inspire you
- Your physical world
- The resources you have available
- Health and wellbeing

DAILY MINDSET RITUAL

Start each day with at least 5 things you are thankful for and end the day with at least 5 things that have gone well with your day.

Appreciation Rampage

DAY 2

Mind the Gap

Today is all about taking the first steps towards clarity on what you truly want, and the best way to do that is to look at the areas of your life where you currently feel in lack or discomfort.

We are usually taught not to focus on what we lack, because we'll simply manifest more of it. BUT, taking note of where you feel the most discomfort is the best indicator of what you truly want.

I don't want you to spend too long focusing on what you don't have, but allow yourself to feel any 'negative' feelings and then ask your intuition to guide you to what you desire.

Here are some journaling prompts that can help you:
- What am I currently lacking in my life?
- What feels uncomfortable/frustrating/like I'm stuck?
- How would I like this situation to look and feel instead?
- What could I manifest that would change this void?
- What would flow look and feel like in this area?

Today I am grateful for:

Mind the Gap

DAY 3

Your Ideal Day

This is one of my FAVOURITE tools for helping you to get clarity on your true desires AND attract them. It's simple but amazingly powerful.

Write in great detail about your ideal day. What time would you get up, where would you be, what would you do first, who would you be spending time with, what would you wear, what would you eat, etc.

Write in as much detail as possible and include how every aspect of this day will make you feel.

Important Note – Stay away from the word 'should'. Don't include anything that feels like a chore, or anything that you think you **should** *be doing.*

Let your mind wander and your imagination take over as you write about how you'd love to spend 24 hours. Listen to your heart and let your soul guide you to what it desires.

If you find this task hard to do at first, don't stress, remember this is supposed to feel fun. Simply revisit it over the next few days with the intention to discover your true ideal day, and let your intuition take over.

DAILY MINDSET RITUAL

If you love this exercise then add it to your daily mindset ritual, or if you'd prefer, when you know you've got to your true ideal day, simply read through what you've written every day or even every week. Each time you write or read about you ideal day, lean into the feelings and let your heart be filled with excitement and happiness.

Today I am grateful for

My ideal day

DAY 4

Affirmation: the Universe Is Always Supporting Me

This affirmation is so powerful to open you up to receive support and guidance from the Universe.

Your task for today is to repeat this affirmation every hour (I like to use the alarm on my phone to remind me) for the entire day and start to feel, and see, the shifts that happen in your everyday life.

DAILY MINDSET RITUAL

Add this affirmation to your morning journaling practice and place it in various places around your home or digital life. Here are some of my favourite:
- Screensaver on your phone/laptop
- Post-it notes on your mirror/fridge/inside of cupboards
- Reminders on your phone
- Ask Alexa to remind you

However you choose to read/say/hear the affirmation, the important part is to pause for a moment and feel the sensation of being supported.

Today I am grateful for

My empowering affirmations

My ideal day

DAY 5

Lean into the Feelings

The Law of Attraction states that like energy attracts like energy, so the key to manifesting is to get into vibrational alignment with that which you desire.

That means thinking AND feeling how you'll think and feel when what you desire is in your physical reality BEFORE it is.

The best way to do this is to visualise, or imagine, having it now, and focus your thoughts and feelings on your enjoyment of the experience.

The better you FEEL the more you are in alignment and in manifesting flow.

Find 10 minutes today to sit in quiet meditation / visualisation and imagine your world with what you desire in it. Then really feel the excitement / gratitude / joy / pride, etc. that manifestation will bring.

When you've completed your visualisation, bring those feelings with you into the rest of your day and lean into them as much as possible.

Today I am grateful for

My empowering affirmations

My ideal day

DAY 6

Feel the Joy, Raise Your Vibration

Remember yesterday that I said the better you feel, the more in alignment you'll be? Well today's task is all about helping you to feel good more of the time and raise your vibe.

Today I want you to create a list of things that bring YOU joy and happiness.

Include as wide a variety of things as you can. Think everything from a song that makes you feel good to going on holiday (and everything in between).

This task has two purposes:

1. Make the commitment to add more of the things that bring you happiness into your everyday life. Some of these things might be small shifts, others might be bigger, the aim is that your daily life should include more of what you love. Don't get overwhelmed and try to change everything all at once! Start with one thing and then add in others as you go.
2. Use this list as your first port of call if you find yourself lacking motivation, feeling resistance, frustration, or generally feel a bit down. Pick something off your list and do it to get back into a higher vibe.

DAILY MINDSET RITUAL

Do at least one thing every day that brings you immense joy and happiness.

Today I am grateful for

My empowering affirmations

My ideal day

My joyful list

DAY 7

Create Your Vision Board

Now you have some clarity on what you desire AND on how having that will make you feel, it's time to create a vision board.

A vision board is a great tool to help keep you focused on what you want to manifest, and lean into the feelings.

Gather together images, picture, phrases, and words that represent what you want to manifest and the feelings associated with that, then put them all together on either a board, wall, or cupboard door. You could also create a collage for your PC desktop, or a Pinterest board.

I also like to include images or words that remind me of my 'Why' and positive affirmations (such as 'The Universe is always supporting me') to give me a motivational boost when I look at it.

Once your board(s) is complete make sure it's somewhere you'll see it often, and as with the affirmations, when you see it pause and lean into the feelings of those things being your reality.

Today I am grateful for

My empowering affirmations

To bring me joy today I will

My ideal day

DAY 8

Create and Commit to Your Manifesting List

Today's task is all about creating your list of what you want to manifest. Use the tasks we've done in the first 7 days to write a list of things that you want to manifest in the next 6 months, 12 months, 2 years.

Pick a timescale and number of things that works for you.
For example:

In the next 6 months it's this or better:
£15,000 cash; 5 new 1:1 ideal clients; A luxury trip to the Maldives

Only write things on your manifesting list that are a direct reflection on your authentic desires. Be specific on the details that genuinely **matter** but remember to stay flexible and open.

When it comes to co-creation, the Universe works by giving you the opportunities, inspired ideas, connections, and resources to bring into your reality what you desire. My experience is that the chain of events that leads to something becoming your physical reality is never a way that you'd expect or even imagine, so don't worry about the how.

The how is the Universe's job, and she is far more clever than we are, which is why your manifesting list should always include the phrase 'this or better' because you'll most likely receive what you desire in bigger and better ways than you could imagine.

Your job is to stay open to guidance, and take inspired action – more of this to come later in the 28 days.

DAILY MINDSET RITUAL

Write your Manifesting List every day, ideally after your gratitude journaling and the affirmation 'The Universe is always supporting me'.

Today I am grateful for

My manifesting list

My empowering affirmations

To bring me joy today I will

My ideal day

DAY 9

Clear the Clutter

Now you have clarity on what you desire, it's time to make space in your life for it. Decluttering and clearing are really important parts of the manifesting process because they will give you a good foundation to manifest from, otherwise you might find yourself repeating old patterns.

Today is all about the physical clutter in your life and home.

Everything in the known Universe is energy, and clutter is the physical manifestation of unmade decisions and procrastination. All that unnecessary 'stuff' that you're holding onto is literally stagnant energy causing a block to receiving what you want.

Nature hates a vacuum, so your task for today is to start the clearing process; I want you to pick an area of your home, office, or car that feels the most cluttered and commit to clear it. Think of decluttering in a holistic sense – sort, tidy, do, clean, donate, sell and/or upcycle things that you don't want to take with you into your next level life.

If you struggle with decluttering and letting go, re-frame this process as an exciting step towards your dreams rather than a chore I've said you should do. This really is the start of you consciously creating the life you truly want to live.

NOTE: Don't get overwhelmed and think you need to do everything today or even this week! This is a process, tackle it one step at a time and watch the magic unfold in your life as you clear more and more of what you no longer need.

DAILY MINDSET RITUAL

If your home, office, and/or car feel cluttered, commit to 10 minutes of decluttering each day.

Today I am grateful for

Today I will declutter

My manifesting list

My empowering affirmations

To bring me joy today I will

My ideal day

DAY 10

Let Go of What Is No Longer Serving You

Yesterday we looked at physical clutter and starting the process of clearing unnecessary energy from your physical environment. Today is all about looking at the limiting beliefs that are holding you back, so you can change them for supportive and empowering beliefs.

These journaling questions will help you start to uncover the thoughts that are no longer serving you:

- Do I believe it is possible for me to manifest what is on my Manifesting List?
- What is getting in the way of me co-creating the life I want?
- How am I holding myself back?

Be really honest with yourself but don't be judgemental. Awareness is always the step towards changing any negative habit, including limiting beliefs.

Over the next few days I'll be sharing the tools to create new empowering thoughts and build your faith in the Universe. The first is a simple Full Moon Ritual.

The full moon is thought to be a great time to release and clear, and this simple ritual will allow you to let go of what is no longer serving you.

Write down the thoughts, doubts, worries, and limiting beliefs that are holding you back and then go outside once the moon is out, give thanks to Mother Earth and the Universe for their divine support and guidance, and then safely burn the piece of paper.

The 2020 Full Moon Dates are:

10th January
9th February
9th March
8th April
7th May
5th June
3rd August
2nd September
1st October
31st October (BLUE MOON)
30th November
30th December

The 2021 Full Moon Dates are:

28th January
27th February
28th March
27th April
26th May
24th June
24th July
22nd August
21st September
20th October
19th November
19th December

Today I am grateful for

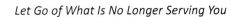

Today I will declutter

My manifesting list

My empowering affirmations

To bring me joy today I will

My ideal day

Uncovering my hidden limiting beliefs

DAY 11

Show Your Resistance Some Love

When something in our life feels negative or unsupportive, our first instinct is to try to push it away or get away from it as quickly as possible. But limiting beliefs, negative thoughts, and doubts have something to teach us about what we need to heal or learn.

Love opens up a space for miracles to happen, so today is all about changing your perspective on the things that have up till now been holding you back.

Re-write the list of limiting beliefs and negative thoughts that came up for you yesterday (any that you can't remember may well have already been released during your full moon ritual). Pick the one that feels as though it's causing you the biggest block and say this prayer:

"Today I choose to see {insert limiting belief / negative thought} through the lens of love. I am open to guidance and support to release this non-supportive pattern and I welcome healing".

And then be truly open to guidance and support to heal and change it.

Guidance might come from your intuition, a social media post, a book recommendation, or an introduction to the perfect person to help you. If it resonates, trust it and allow yourself to start the journey to healing.

Today I am grateful for

_____

Today I will declutter

_____

My manifesting list

My empowering affirmations

To bring me joy today I will

My ideal day

Seeing my limiting beliefs through the lens of love

DAY 12

Journaling Prompt:
Write Your Empowering Story

This exercise is a brilliant tool to help you shift negative beliefs and doubt so you can step into your power. It is similar to the 'Ideal Day' exercise only this time the focus is on you.

This is not thinking that who you are right now isn't good enough or that you need to become someone else, this is you stepping into your authentic goddess self; that inspiring, powerful woman who is not held back by fear and worry. The woman who is driven by passion, purpose, and creating impact.

Here are some ideas to get you started:
- How do you show up in your business?
- How do you lead your team or tribe?
- How do you create content for social media?
- How do you attract new clients?
- How do you tackle challenges?
- What kind of impact do you make for your clients/customers?
- How do you want to show up for your children/partner/family?

Let your mind wander to see that empowering and inspiring vision of your authentic self.

NOTE: Don't get caught in the 'shoulds', include only things that are in alignment with your authentic self, make you feel unstoppable, and truly light you up.

DAILY MINDSET RITUAL

Add your empowering story to your daily journaling practice.

Today I am grateful for

Today I will declutter

My manifesting list

My empowering affirmations

To bring me joy today I will

My ideal day

My empowering story

DAY 13

Affirmation: I Am an Amazing Manifestor

Belief in your ability to manifest is one of the most powerful shifts you can make.

This affirmation will help you to lean into that belief and your task for today is to repeat this affirmation every hour (I like to use the alarm on my phone to remind me) for the entire day and start to feel, and see, the shifts that happen in your everyday life.

We are also going to go one step further to really anchor and strengthen this belief.

As well as repeating this affirmation I want you to create a list of the things in your life you have already manifested, and the times when you feel as though you've been supported by the Universe.

Remember that the Law of Attraction is working all the time so you may have manifested things in the past without consciously trying to do so!

Think about all the times things just seem to have fallen into place, all the times you've got exactly what you asked for really easily, and the times when coincidences have been super helpful.

DAILY MINDSET RITUAL

Add this affirmation to 'The Universe is always supporting me' as part of your daily mindset ritual.

Today I am grateful for

Today I will declutter

My manifesting list

My empowering affirmations

To bring me joy today I will

My ideal day

My empowering story

DAY 14

Journaling Prompt: If I Had Full Faith that What I Wanted Was on its Way, How Would I Think, Act and Feel?

The secret to successful manifesting is being able to think, feel, and act as though what you desire is already in your physical reality, before it arrives.

One trap lots of people fall into is focusing on the WANT for what they are trying to manifest rather than HAVING it.

The difference might seem subtle but the effect is massive.

Let's take money as an example. If you're focusing on the want for money, you are going to attract situations into your life where you WANT more money. This could manifest as unexpected bills, a parking ticket, or a course you'd love to do but feel you can't afford.

When you switch your focus to how you will feel WHEN you have more money in your life BEFORE it shows up, your point of attraction is abundance. What you'll start to manifest is opportunities to earn more, new clients might appear as if from nowhere, and even unexpected windfalls.

This journaling question will help you to tap into the thoughts, feelings, and actions of having what you desire so you can lean into them now.

Today I am grateful for

Today I will declutter

My manifesting list

My empowering affirmations

To bring me joy today I will

My ideal day

My empowering story

If I had full faith, I would...

DAY 15

Let Go of the 'How' and Your Expectations

Do you find yourself trying to think through every detail of how your desired manifestation is going to arrive, over planning the results, or clinging on to expectations of how something is going to turn out?

The Universe is so much cleverer than we are and she has a plan far greater than our own. Surrender is all about handing over your goals and dreams, knowing that you will be guided to achieve them in ways that go beyond your current thinking.

The first tool to help you surrender is this simple prayer:

"Today I surrender my dreams and goals with full faith that I will receive this or better. I accept spiritual guidance knowing that where there were challenges and blocks there will be opportunities, solutions, and creative ideas. I step back from my own agenda and commit to taking aligned action from a place of gratitude, abundance, and faith."

DAILY MINDSET RITUAL

Add this prayer to your daily journaling practice to make surrender a daily practice

Today I am grateful for

Today I will declutter

My manifesting list

My empowering affirmations

To bring me joy today I will

My ideal day

My empowering story

DAY 16

Hand Over Your Goals

As we continue the theme of surrender, this beautiful meditation will help you to hand over your goals to the care of a power far greater than yourself.

Sit comfortably either cross-legged on the floor, or in a chair.
If you wish, you can have some relaxing music playing quietly in the background.
Close your eyes and focus your attention on your breathing.
Breath in slowly through your nose allowing air to fill your lungs, hold for a moment, then exhale slowly.
Repeat this breathing long and deep, and feel your body relax.
Feeling calm and centred, imagine a beautiful basket filled with soft light appearing in front of you.
Now imagine yourself placing your dreams and goals, either written on paper or as pictures, into this basket.
As you do so let love, gratitude, and excitement fill your body because you know that surrendering your desires means they are on the way.
With all your dreams safely in the basket, it slowly disappears into a bright stream of light.
Sit with the feelings this meditation brings for as long as you wish.
When you're ready, slowly come back into your body and open your eyes.

Today I am grateful for

_____
_____
_____
_____
_____
_____
_____
_____
_____
_____
_____
_____

Today I will declutter

_____
_____
_____
_____

My manifesting list

My empowering affirmations

To bring me joy today I will

My ideal day

My empowering story

DAY 17

Action Prompt: Get the Nest Ready

The last few days' tasks have all focused on surrendering your goals to the loving guidance of the Universe, and today is all about starting to ACT AS IF.

This isn't a 'fake it till you make it' thing, this is acting as your authentic future self who has already manifested your desires. This is such a powerful signal to the Universe that you have full faith and are ready to receive.

Today's task is all about getting the nest ready. What would you do to prepare if you knew that what you wanted was going to appear today or tomorrow?

Ideas include:
- Blocking out time in your diary
- Getting new client files ready
- Booking the trip and paying a deposit
- Planning the programme before anyone books on
- Booking a venue for the event you want to run
- Announcing a release date for your book

Today is about getting into positive action because the magic happens when the Law of Attraction meets the Law of Action.

Today I am grateful for

My manifesting list

My empowering affirmations

To bring me joy today I will

My ideal day

My empowering story

To get the nest ready I can

DAY 18

Money Gratitude List

Over the next few days we are going to be focusing specifically on manifesting money, because so many of the things you desire can either come into your life with an increase in abundance, or will be supported by having more money.

Money can get a bed reputation and many people struggle with limiting money beliefs and a lack mindset. The tasks over the next 4 days will help you to adopt feelings of gratitude and abundance to change your point of money attraction.

Today's task is all about leaning into the feelings of gratitude for money specifically, because what you are grateful for grows in your life.

Write a list of EVERYTHING that you are grateful to money for and remember that money is in almost everything.

DAILY MINDSET RITUAL

Either add in a specific money gratitude to your daily gratitude practice or focus entirely on money gratitude for the next few days.

Today I am grateful for

Today I will declutter

My manifesting list

My empowering affirmations

To bring me joy today I will

My ideal day

Money Gratitude list

My empowering story

DAY 19

Track Your Income with Gratitude

"Energy Flows Where Attention Goes", so tracking every bit of money that comes to you is a great practical tool to create an abundance mindset.

This isn't for accounting purposes but is just a simple way of saying a daily 'thank you' and keeping your focus on the money that is flowing **TO** you.

At the end of each day make a note of the money that you have received. This could be income, interest, cash back, unexpected tax refund, money you find on the street, etc. Also track any 'value' you have received; unexpected discounts, vouchers you've used, even when a friend has bought you a coffee.

It's all abundance that is flowing to you.

DAILY MINDSET RITUAL

Track the money that flows to you at the end of each day.

Today I am grateful for

Today I will declutter

My manifesting list

My empowering affirmations

To bring me joy today I will

My ideal day

My empowering story

Money I have received today

DAY 20

Write Yourself a Cheque

If you've not heard the 'Jim Carrey's $10 million cheque' story, here's a brief recount:

'Jim was a struggling actor in Hollywood, getting turned down for job after job and struggling to pay the bills. He would spend his evenings sitting overlooking LA, visualising directors that he wanted to work with saying "Yes", and being asked to star in dream projects. The whole time Jim was telling himself that they were out there, he just didn't have hold of them yet.

He wrote himself a cheque for $10,000,000 for acting services rendered, dated it 3 years in the future, and carried it with him in his wallet.

Days before the date on the cheque he signed the contract to star in 'Dumb and Dumber', for which he was paid $10,000,000.'

Today's task is to write yourself a cheque (you can download a cheque template if you no longer own a cheque book) for a dream amount of money you want to receive and the date by which you want to have it. Then put it somewhere you'll see it multiple times a day and every time you see it, feel gratitude and excitement that the money is on its way to you.

Today I am grateful for

Today I will declutter

My manifesting list

My empowering affirmations

To bring me joy today I will

My ideal day

My empowering story

_____

_____

_____

_____

_____

_____

_____

_____

_____

_____

_____

_____

_____

_____

Money I have received today

_____

_____

_____

_____

_____

DAY 21

Energetic Spending

This is one of my favourite tools to help you create an abundance mindset, and is particularly helpful if you find yourself slipping into the 'I can't afford it' story.

Have an amount of money – £50 is a good amount (especially if you can get hold of a £50 note) that you have designated for energetic spending. Have this money, as cash, in your purse at all times.

Throughout your day, as you see things that you like, remind yourself that you have money ready and available to spend.

For example:
"That dress is beautiful and I have the money to buy it."
"I have the money to buy those earrings."
"I have the money available to fill my car with fuel."
"If I choose, I can buy all those books in one go."

The idea of this exercise isn't to *actually* buy the things, but to tell yourself you can. You don't physically spend the money, you spend it *energetically* over and over again each day.

DAILY MINDSET RITUAL

Energetically spend your £50 at least 10 times per day. It's a really fun way to create an abundance mindset.

Today I am grateful for

Today I will declutter

My manifesting list

My empowering affirmations

To bring me joy today I will

My ideal day

My empowering story

Money I have received today

DAY 22

Release Any Resentment

Are you holding onto resentment about anything?

There are times in life when we all experience things that feel unfair; for example, being passed over for a promotion, or a potential new client choosing the competition instead. But resentment is an energetic block and pushes away what you're trying to attract.

It's time to release any resentment that you might be holding on to, and this simple prayer will help you to shift your perspective and be open to any healing or learning.

"Today I choose to release the resentment about {insert event here} that I've been holding on to. I see that this energy no longer serves me and I am ready to understand what I can learn from this situation, what I need to heal, and where I am ready to grow."

Today I am grateful for

_____

_____

_____

_____

_____

_____

_____

_____

Today I will declutter

_____

_____

_____

My manifesting list

My empowering affirmations

To bring me joy today I will

What resentment am I holding onto?

My ideal day

My empowering story

Money I have received today

DAY 23

Affirmation: I am Worthy of Everything that I Desire

The final part of our 28 day manifesting journey is to building worthiness and be open to receive. What you manifest into your life is a direct reflection on what you believe you are worthy of. If you struggle with confidence and self-belief it will cause energetic resistance.

If you want to manifest something that, right now, you believe you are not worthy of having, all you will bring into your life is more situations and circumstances that reflect your lack self-worthiness. This could be potential clients saying no to you, being turned down for your dream job, etc.

You have to do the mindset work first. You have to think, feel and act as though what you desire is already yours, and that includes believing that you deserve it AND can have it.

This affirmation is the perfect place to start to create that mindset shift. As with the other affirmations, write it, read it, set reminders, and put it on sticky notes around your house.

I AM WORTHY OF EVERYTHING THAT I DESIRE

DAILY MINDSET RITUAL

Add this affirmation to your daily mindset practice to start building the belief that you are worthy of everything you desire.

Today I am grateful for

Today I will declutter

My manifesting list

My empowering affirmations

To bring me joy today I will

My ideal day

My empowering story

Money I have received today

DAY 24

Use Your Best Things

Today's task is really simple but really powerful in building your belief that you are worthy of the good stuff.

Having things in your life that you don't allow yourself to use and enjoy simply reinforces the negative belief that you're not worthy

You **do** deserve to wear lovely perfume every day.

You **do** deserve to write in the special journal you've been keeping for a rainy day.

You **do** deserve the effort of making a proper coffee every day.

Last year I treated myself to a beautiful hand-painted china tea cup, and then never used it! It just sat there in my cupboard whilst I used the cheap mugs I've had for years. Now I used it every day and when I do, it feels like I'm having a really special treat AND the tea tastes better.

Life is precious, simply being here is the special occasion and you deserve the best every day.

Today I am grateful for

Today I will declutter

My manifesting list

My empowering affirmations

To bring me joy today I will

My ideal day

My empowering story

Money I have received today

DAY 25

Upgrade One Area of Your Life

Today's task I learned from the amazing Denise Duffield Thomas and is a brilliant way to help you to continue building your feelings of worthiness. After starting to use your 'best' things yesterday, today is all about upgrading one area of your life where you currently allow yourself less than you deserve. This could be using an old dining chair in your office that gives you backache instead of investing in a new office chair with proper lumbar support, or maybe it's always buying the cheapest soap when actually you'd love to use an artisan hand crafted soap.

Maybe you're still wearing the bras you bought 10 years ago that are faded and fit poorly, but you keep thinking they'll do.

This isn't about living beyond your current means, this is identifying *one* area of your life where you are not allowing yourself what you are worthy of, and upgrading it to what you truly desire and deserve.

NOTE: It's okay to start with small things; you do deserve the premium bath salts or the notebook with the beautiful cover. This is about starting to tell yourself that you are worthy of the best.

Today I am grateful for

Today I will declutter

My manifesting list

_____

_____

_____

_____

_____

_____

My empowering affirmations

_____

_____

_____

_____

To bring me joy today I will

_____

_____

_____

_____

My ideal day

My empowering story

_____

_____

_____

_____

_____

_____

_____

_____

_____

_____

_____

_____

_____

Money I have received today

_____

_____

_____

_____

DAY 26

Infinite Patience Brings Immediate Results

This is one of my favourite quotes by Wayne Dyer because it sums up beautifully the paradox that is surrendering to manifesting flow.

When you hand over what you desire with full faith, the Universe works quickly.

But impatience and a lack of faith lead to trying to control the outcome and force your manifestation into reality, which only serves as a block.

Remember that I said when you think you've surrendered, surrender some more?

Today's task is to check in with yourself and ask:
- Have I fully surrendered my desire?
- Do I have full faith that it's on its way?
- Do I have infinite patience?

If the answer is 'no' then it's time to dig a little deeper to discover the root cause of this block. Remember that everything in nature has a gestation period and patience removes energetic resistance.

Today I am grateful for

Today I will declutter

My manifesting list

My empowering affirmations

To bring me joy today I will

Surrendered check in

My ideal day

My empowering story

Money I have received today

DAY 27

Take Aligned, Inspired Action

You know what you want, you've cleared resistance, you believe you are worthy of it and that it's possible for you to have. Now it's time to get into aligned and inspired action.

The secret to successful and speedy manifesting is learning to act as if you cannot fail to manifest your desires.

You may have already had an inspired idea that will move you forward – those flashes of inspiration and bright ideas are gifts and guidance from the Universe. Learn to trust them and act on them.

If you're unsure what to do, try one of these:

Set a powerful intention – Set the intention of what you want to achieve and then keep your eyes, ears, and mind open.

Ask for guidance – Ask the Universe to guide you foward to the next inspired action and then trust the guidance when you receive it. Usually it comes via an inspired idea or an intuitive knowing but guidance can come in more practical forms like meeting the perfect person to help you with something you've been struggling with.

Today I am grateful for

Today I will declutter

My manifesting list

My empowering affirmations

To bring me joy today I will

Today's inspired action

My ideal day

My empowering story

Money I have received today

DAY 28

Affirmation:
I am Open and Willing to Receive

Congratulations! You have reached the final day of this manifesting journal, but this is just the start of your journey co-creating with the Universe.

Your final task is to embody this affirmation that you are open and willing to receive all that you desire. As with the other affirmations, write, read, and speak this multiple times a day, pausing each time to really feel what it means to be open and willing to receive.

Today I am grateful for

Today I will declutter

My manifesting list

My empowering affirmations

To bring me joy today I will

Today's inspired action

My ideal day

My empowering story

Money I have received today

DAY 29 and Beyond

Miracles and effortless manifesting are your birthright, yet it's remarkably easy to block the positive flow with limiting beliefs, energetic resistance, negative thoughts, and a lack of faith.

If you've consistently used the daily tools of the last 28 days you will have already felt the magical shift in your mindset and you may also have seen some shifts in your outer world as well.

Remember that the Law of Attraction is working all the time and your life is a direct reflection of your inner state. Don't let this overwhelm or worry you. You now have the tools to ensure that it is working for you. Learning to co-create with the Universe is a fun, exciting and sometimes surprising, journey.

"The quality of your life is the quality of your habits" – Rachel Hollis

Commit to your daily mindset ritual. Remembering that your mindset is a muscle and the biggest shifts happen from the small consistent mindset work that you do each day. Believe in your heart that you are meant for a life of purpose, abundance, fulfilment, and miracles.

"Infinite patience produces an immediate result" – A Course in Miracles

Everything in nature has a gestation period, a time of silent growth when it looks to the outside world like nothing is changing, but really it's all happening beneath the surface.

Learn to relax about how things are going to happen, lean into the idea that what you want may come out of the blue and in a way you can't yet imagine. Start to believe that amazing and unexpected things are coming your way and that you are the sort of person who always gets the lucky breaks and the fortunate coincidences and you will be.

Be open to receive and follow your intuition, and do what feels right on a soul level, even when it seems off the wall. The Universe works fast when you're having fun!

And finally, relax, have fun, and enjoy the process. Raise your vibe by making gratitude and happiness your default, stay in alignment by focusing on the feelings of already having what you desire and enjoy the beautiful process of co-creating your dream life with the Universe.

Ready for even more? If this journal has opened a door for you and you're ready for your next level, visit www.emmakatedawson.com for lots more resources and all the information on the ways I can help and support you on a deeper and more personal level.

Happy Manifesting!

Light and Love,
Emma

DAY 30

Today I am grateful for

Today I will declutter

My manifesting list

My empowering affirmations

To bring me joy today I will

Today's inspired action

My ideal day

My empowering story

Money I have received today

DAY 31

Today I am grateful for

Today I will declutter

My manifesting list

My empowering affirmations

To bring me joy today I will

Today's inspired action

My ideal day

My empowering story

Money I have received today

DAY 32

Today I am grateful for

Today I will declutter

My manifesting list

My empowering affirmations

To bring me joy today I will

Today's inspired action

My ideal day

My empowering story

Money I have received today

DAY 33

Today I am grateful for

Today I will declutter

My manifesting list

My empowering affirmations

To bring me joy today I will

Today's inspired action

My ideal day

My empowering story

Money I have received today

DAY 34

Today I am grateful for

Today I will declutter

My manifesting list

My empowering affirmations

To bring me joy today I will

Today's inspired action

My ideal day

My empowering story

Money I have received today

DAY 35

Today I am grateful for

Today I will declutter

My manifesting list

_____

_____

_____

_____

_____

_____

My empowering affirmations

_____

_____

_____

To bring me joy today I will

_____

_____

_____

Today's inspired action

My ideal day

My empowering story

Money I have received today

DAY 36

Today I am grateful for

Today I will declutter

My manifesting list

My empowering affirmations

To bring me joy today I will

Today's inspired action

My ideal day

My empowering story

Money I have received today

Printed in Great Britain
by Amazon